Bible
Study
made
easy

Mark Water

HUNT&
THORPE

OM
publishing

Copyright © 1998 Hunt & Thorpe
Text copyright © 1998 Mark Water

Unless otherwise indicated, scripture
quotations are taken from the HOLY BIBLE,
NEW INTERNATIONAL VERSION, copyright
© 1973, 1978, 1984 by International Bible
Society. All rights reserved.

ISBN 1 85608 386 1

Designed and produced
by Tony Cantale Graphics

Photography supplied by
Goodshoot, Digital Vision and
Tony Cantale

Illustrations by
Tony Cantale Graphics

Write to:
Hunt & Thorpe, Laurel House,
Station Approach, New Alresford,
Hampshire SO24 9JH, UK.

Hunt & Thorpe is a name used under
licence by Paternoster Publishing,
PO Box 300, Kingstown Broadway,
Carlisle CA3 0QW, UK

The right of Mark Water to be
identified as the author of this work
has been asserted by him in
accordance with the Copyright,
Designs and Patents Act 1988.

A CIP catalogue record for this book
is available from the British Library.

Manufactured In Hong Kong / China

Contents

Special pull-out chart

A bird's-eye view of Bible books and themes

Which Bible version should I use?

Use a Bible

Beg, borrow or buy a Bible.

You can borrow a Bible from a library.

You will need to use your Bible as you follow through each study in this book.

Which Bible version should I use?

There are scores of different Bible versions to choose from in bookstores. They fall into two categories:

- **Translations.** Great attention is paid to translating the exact meaning of each Greek or Hebrew word or phrase.
- **Paraphrases.** These may add or omit words in order to communicate the original meaning in the most helpful and arresting way.

J.B. Phillips' version of Romans 12:2 is a good example of an excellent paraphrase:

"Don't let the world around you squeeze you into its own mould, but let God re-make you so that your whole attitude of mind is changed."

Six versions of John 3:16 compared

King James Version	New Revised Standard Version	Today's English Version
For God so loved the world, that he gave his only begotten Son, that whosoever believeth in him should not perish, but have everlasting life.	For God so loved the world that he gave his only Son, that whoever believes in him should not perish but have eternal life.	For God loved the world so much he gave his only Son, so that everyone who believes in him may not die but have eternal life.

Inclusive language

Some Bibles published in the 1990s now have "'inclusive" language editions. Direct translations of the Bible may appear sexist to modern readers, with references to "man" or to "brothers." Inclusive language editions use the words "human beings" and "brothers and sisters."

Bible reference	Traditional translation	NRSV inclusive language
Matthew 4:19	"I will make you fishers of men."	"I will make you fishers of men and women."
1 Thessalonians 5:25-26	"Brothers, pray for us. Greet all the brothers with a holy kiss."	"Brothers and sisters, pray for us. Greet all God's people with a holy kiss."

The choice is yours

There has never been a wider variety of good translations from which to choose.

New Living (translation)
For God loved the world so much that he gave his only Son so that anyone who believes in him shall not perish but have eternal life.

The Message (paraphrase)
For God loved the world so much that he gave his only Son, so that everyone who believes in him should not be lost, but should have eternal life.

New International Version
For God so loved the world that he gave his one and only Son, that whoever believes in him shall not perish but have everlasting life.

Making a start

Mastering Bible references

Breaking down what is meant by the code **1 John 3:16** is easy.
• **1** means John's first letter (John wrote three letters).
• **John** is the name of the Bible book.
• The first figure after the name of the Bible book, in this case **3**, is the chapter number.
• The figure after the colon, in this case **16**, is the verse number.
So **1 John 3:16** is John's first letter, chapter 3, verse 16.

Finding Bible books

But where exactly does John's first letter come in the Bible? The easiest way to find any Bible book is to go to the front of the Bible. Here books are listed, often both in Bible order and in alphabetical order, with the page number next to the Bible book.

To get the most out of Bible study, look up all the Bible references in this book. Think of it as an exciting way to explore your Bible for yourself.

Give it a try

Try looking up John 3:16 and 1 John 3:16. This is not a catch! John 3:16 is not one of John's letters, but his gospel, known to us as John's Gospel. But 1 John 3:16, as we've just seen, is from John's first letter. Look up both verses, and you'll see that amazingly, they have a common theme.

How's your memory?

Try memorizing John 3:16. Bring it to mind during the day. See if you can remember it at the end of the day. Then do the same for 1 John 3:16.

You will now have done what you are told to do in Psalm 119:11!

Pray before you start

A version of Psalm 119:18 is used as a prayer by many people as they start to read the Bible.

> "Open my eyes [that is, my spiritual understanding] that I may see wonderful things in your law. Amen."

Remember, the main point of Bible study is not to acquire knowledge, but to get acquainted with God and his purpose for you.

Think

Praying and turning things over in our minds are complementary activities. We are meant to use our God-given faculties to the fullest when we read the Bible.

How to cope with difficult passages

Don't be put off by parts that are hard to understand. This is the best way to deal with them. Always ask God to send his Holy Spirit to illuminate the passage for you. Write down the Bible reference, and jot down your question. Then ask an experienced Christian, or read a reference book about the passage. When you do find the answer, be sure to write it down next to your question. Over the course of a year, you'll be very pleasantly surprised at how many of your questions have been answered!

Boredom

Many people give up reading and studying the Bible through sheer boredom. This is because they are reading the Bible as an abstract exercise. Look at your Bible reading as an adventure – an opportunity to know God, and his Son Jesus Christ. Each time you read your Bible, ask God to show you how to take action on what you have read – then do it. Help to counteract boredom by giving yourself plenty of variety, in reading different parts of the Bible.

7

See also:
• *Questions to ask*, page 10
• *15 ways to enhance your Bible study*, page 64.

Nine ways NOT to study the Bible

The Bible is the most wonderful book in the world.
But sadly, it has often been misused and misquoted.

The mistake	The solution
Taking a text out of its context. An example of this is comes in Genesis 4:9: "Am I my brother's keeper?" Some have quoted these words to mean that we should not be concerned with other people's welfare.	**A text out of context is a pretext.** The words in Genesis 4:9 are words spoken by Cain, who has just murdered his brother Abel! Cain lies to God, saying he does not know where Abel is. The point is that we are meant to be our "brother's keeper."
Interpreting a poetic image in a literal way. This has led to dreadful persecution, as Galileo would tell you! For example, take Psalm 93:1, which says: "The world is firmly established; it cannot be moved." For hundreds of years some Christians thought that anyone who did not believe that the earth was fixed, and the sun went round it, was a heretic.	**Interpret poetic language as poetry.** The first half of Psalm 93:1 states: "The Lord reigns, he is robed in majesty; the Lord is robed in majesty and is armed with strength." The psalm is about God's majesty and power: it is not meant to teach us about astronomy. Look out of your window. Doesn't the earth seem solid and fixed? The psalmist is saying that God is strong in the same way.
Misquoting a verse. One of the most frequently misquoted verses is 1 Timothy 6:10, which comes out as: "Money is the root of all evil." (This has been taken to mean that money in itself is evil, and that Christians should have nothing to do with it.)	**Make accurate quotations.** 1 Timothy 6:10 actually says, "For the love of money is a root of all kinds of evil." It is the love of money, not money itself which is the problem, as the second half of the verse amplifies: "Some people, eager for money, have wandered away from the faith and pierced themselves with many griefs."
Quoting half a verse. Matthew 22:21, "Give to Caesar what is Caesar's..." is frequently quoted in isolation from the second half of the verse. It emphasizes only a Christian's duty to the State.	**Quote the whole verse.** The second half of Matthew 22:21 reads, "... and to God what is God's." Jesus is saying that we have a dual responsibility: to the State and to God.

Studying only the "nice" verses. Some parts of the Bible make very disturbing reading. Psalm 137:8-9 reads, "Happy is he … who seizes your infants and dashes them against the rocks."	**Face the tough verses head-on.** There may be some verses in the Bible that you do not understand. Do not let these stop you from appreciating the rest that you do understand. When the psalmist cried out for immediate vengeance against evil people, he had no idea of Christ's sacrificial death for sin, or of the future final judgment.
Getting submerged in the Old Testament. Some long passages in the Old Testament might not make much sense to you, and discourage you from reading the Bible. When the British pop star Cliff Richard began to read the Bible, he started at Genesis but gave up when he reached Leviticus because he did not understand what all the sacrifices were about.	**Move from the familiar to the unfamiliar.** If you haven't read the Bible before, start with some of the following key Old Testament passages. • The creation. *Genesis 1:1-2:7* • The fall of man. *Genesis 3:6-24* • The call of Abraham. *Genesis 12:1-9* • The story of Joseph. *Genesis 37-38* • The Ten Commandments. *Exodus 20:1-17* • The shepherd's psalm. *Psalm 23*
Starting with the most difficult New Testament books. If you are not familiar with the New Testament, it is best not to start with the Book of Revelation and the Letter to the Hebrews.	**Start with an overview of the New Testament.** Here are some key New Testament passages. • The birth of Jesus. *Luke 1:26-2:40* • The Sermon on the Mount. *Matthew 5-7* • The prodigal son. *Luke 15:11-32* • The Last Supper. *Matthew 26:20-25* • The death and resurrection of Jesus. *John 19-20* • The conversion of Paul. *Acts 9:1-31* • The life of joy. *Paul's Letter to the Philippians*
Not acting on the Bible's commands	**Obedience is crucial** "Be doers of the word, and not hearers only." *James 1:22 (NRSV)*
Using the Bible as a battleground for fruitless arguments	**Avoid arguing over unimportant things** *See Titus 3:9*

Questions to ask

When Jesus met people, he often asked them questions.
When we read the Bible, one of the best ways to increase our
understanding about a passage is to ask questions about it.

General questions

There are some general questions which are well worth asking
of any Bible passage. Some people find it helpful to have a
notepad in which they write down all their questions, and the
answers they discover.
• What have I learned about God the Father?
• What have I learned about Jesus?
• What have I learned about the Holy Spirit?
• Did I find a good example to follow?
• Is there a promise to believe in the passage?
• Is there a command to obey?

Looking at a specific Bible passage

You will need to ask different questions about different
passages. Here are some questions to ask about the opening
verses of a Bible book which some people find very hard to
understand – the Book of Revelation.

Bible passage

(1) The revelation of Jesus Christ, which God gave him to show his servants what must soon take place. He made it known by sending his angel to his servant John, (2) who testifies to everything he saw – that is, the word of God and the testimony of Jesus Christ. (3) Blessed is the one who reads the words of this prophecy, and blessed are those who hear it and take to heart what is written in it, because the time is near.
(4) John,
To the seven churches in the province of Asia: Grace and peace to you from him who is, and who was, and who is to come, and from the seven spirits before his throne, (5) and from Jesus Christ, who is the faithful witness, the firstborn from the dead, and the ruler of the kings of the earth.
To him who loves us and has freed us from our sins by his blood, (6) and has made us to be a kingdom and priests to serve his God and Father – to him be glory and power for ever and ever! Amen.
Revelation 1:1-6

Question	Answer
1 Who wrote this book?	See verses 1, 4. See also Revelation 1:9.
2 To whom did John write this book?	See verse 4. Also see Revelation chapters 2-3.
3 What is the theme of the book?	See verse 1.
4 What type of book is this?	See verse 3.
5 What does John want his readers to receive?	See verse 4.
6 In which three ways is Jesus described?	See verse 5. Also see Revelation 1:8.
7 Which three things has Jesus done for us?	See verses 5-6.
8 What directions are we given about how to read this book?	See verse 3. Also see Revelation 22:18-19.
9 What response should we give to God the Father?	See verse 6. See also Revelation 4:6-11.

What are commentaries, concordances, Bible dictionaries, New Testament interlinears?

While there is no substitute for reading the words of the Bible itself, there are many different books to help you in your study of the Bible.

Commentaries

These are books which give systematic comments, observations, and sometimes personal application notes, on different passages of the Bible.

• There are some excellent one-volume Bible commentaries which look at each book of the Bible, from Genesis to Revelation.

• There are commentaries on individual books of the Bible, examining each verse in detail.

Concordances

These are books which enable you to look up almost any word found in the Bible.

• If you were studying the Holy Spirit, you would find dozens of references if you looked up the words **"Spirit"** and **"Holy"** in a Bible concordance.

• If you wanted to find a passage in the Bible about the Good Samaritan, you would look up **"Samaritan"** and find: "But a Samaritan, as he traveled, came where." *Luke 10:33*

• You could see how words are linked together in the Bible. By looking up the occurrence of the word **"grace"** in the New Testament, you would discover that it was most often linked with "peace." *(See Romans 1:7;*

1 Corinthians 1:3; 2 Corinthians 1:2; Galatians 1:3; Ephesians 1:2; Philippians 1:2; Colossians 1:2; 2 Thessalonians 1:2; Titus 1:4; Philemon 3; 1 Peter 1:2; 2 Peter 1:2 and Revelation 1:4.) "Grace and peace to you" was the normal way of starting a letter!

• Other information may be gleaned from the references. For example, you could find out who gives grace, and what the purpose of receiving grace is.

• Bible concordances are linked to a particular translation of the Bible. So if you buy one, make sure that it is based on the Bible version you like using.

Bible Dictionaries

Bible dictionaries are ideal books for looking up individual Bible words, Bible people and Bible themes.

- **Samaria and the Samaritans**
  For example, if you look up the entry under "Samaria," it will not only tell you about the origin of the country of Samaria (the northern kingdom of Israel), but also about Samaritans. In Jesus' time, Samaritans were people of mixed race who were despised by the Jews. When Jesus told the story of the Good Samaritan, he asked his listeners who, in the story, had acted as a neighbor? The man who answered could not even bring himself to say the word "Samaritan," so replied, "The one who had mercy."

New Testament Interlinears

You need to know just a little Greek to benefit from an interlinear Bible. New Testament interlinears set the complete New Testament in Greek, with the literal English translation for each word underneath each line of Greek text. This means that you can see which Greek word is used in a particular verse.

Bible Handbooks

These books are excellent for giving you background information about the Bible, along with a summary of each Bible book. They cover such topics as archeology, minerals, animals and insects, plants and herbs, trades, travel, warfare, money, marriage, childhood, disease and music.

Bible Atlases

Bible atlases are ideal for increasing our understanding of the Bible.

- **From Dan to Beersheba**
  This phrase means from the north to the south. "Then all the Israelites from Dan to Beersheba came." *Judges 20:1*. An atlas shows that Dan was the northernmost city in Israel, while Beersheba was the southernmost city in Israel.

- **Jonah fled to Tarshish**
  God told Jonah to go to Nineveh but he headed for Tarshish. *Jonah 1:1-3*. A Bible atlas reveals Jonah's great disobedience, as Tarshish was hundreds of miles from Nineveh and in the opposite direction.

Looking through a microscope

Opening observations

Thinking about one person, theme, event or word is a most helpful way of studying the Bible.

This study puts the key word "faith" under the microscope.

It is possible to make such a study by tracking down the places where the word comes in the Bible.

A study of the word "faith"

The table on page 15 sets out where the word "faith" occurs frequently in the Bible. The Bible book is followed by the relevant chapter. The verse number refers to the first occurrence of the word in that chapter. You will have to find how many other occurrences exist in the chapter.

By looking up these Bible references, you will have a good overview of the Bible's teaching on faith.

List the various aspects of faith mentioned and the different people who have faith. Note the Bible reference under each topic or person, as you proceed with this study.

> "Faith is being sure of what we hope for and certain of what we do not see." *Hebrews 11:1*

> "I live by faith in the Son of God, who loved me and gave himself for me." *Galatians 2:20*

N.B. Some Bible versions use the words "believe" or "convert" in place of the word "faith."

Book of Bible	Chapter and verse of first occurrence of "faith"	Number of times "faith" comes in this chapter
Hebrews	11:1	29
James	2:5	15
Romans	4:3	16
Galatians	3:6	
1 Timothy	1:2	9
Mark	9:23	4
Romans	3:22	
1 Timothy	6:10	
Romans	14:1	6
1 Thessalonians	3:2	5
1 Peter	1:5	6
Matthew	18:6	
Romans	1:8	
Romans	10:6	8
Luke	17:5	3
1 Corinthians	13:2	2
Galatians	2:16	4
Colossians	2:5	3
1 Timothy	3:6	2
1 Timothy	4:1	6
2 Timothy	1:5	3
2 Timothy	3:8	3
Titus	1:1	6
Hebrews	4:2	1
2 Peter	1:1	2

15

Concluding thought
- At the end of some study Bibles, complete lists of key words are set noted, providing material for hundreds of Bible studies.
- See also: *The telescopic approach to Bible study*, page 16.

The telescopic approach to Bible study

Opening observation

To gain an overview of a long and involved Bible book, it is sometimes best to read it in one sitting. John's Gospel can be read in about an hour.

The purpose of John's Gospel

John tells us why he wrote his gospel:

"Jesus did many other miraculous signs in the presence of his disciples, which are not recorded in this book. But these are written that you may believe that Jesus is the Christ, the Son of God, and that by believing you may have life in his name." *John 20:30-31*

Themes in John's Gospel

It's useful to keep the major themes in mind, as you read John.

Eternal life	John links eternal life with the "new birth" and with the "second birth."	*John 1:4, 12-13; 3:3-7, 16, 36; 5:21, 24-29; 6:27, 40, 47, 54, 57-58, 68; 10:28; 11:25; 12:25, 50; 17:2-3*
The Holy Spirit	John talks more about the Holy Spirit than the other three gospel writers. The Holy Spirit is spoken of as the one who takes the place of Jesus, after Jesus returns to the Father.	*John 1:32-33; 3:5-6, 8, 34; 4:23-24; 6:63; 7:37-39; 14:16-17, 25-26; 16:7-15; 20:22*
Jesus died for sinners	John concentrates on why Jesus had to die, and on the great love which motivated him in this.	*John 1:29, 36; 2:19-22; 3:14-17; 6:51, 53-56; 8:28; 10:11, 15, 18; 11:50-52; 12:24, 27, 32-34; 15:13*

Outline of John's Gospel

Read through John's Gospel again

- This time, watch for the words "belief" and "faith," and words related to them. These words, and associated words, appear nearly 100 times in John's Gospel.

Linking the Old and New Testaments

Jesus' temptation

During Jesus' time of temptation in the desert, he countered the Devil three times with quotations from the Book of Deuteronomy.

The devil's attack	Jesus' defense
"If you are the Son of God, tell these stones to become bread." *Matthew 4:3*	"It is written: 'Man does not live on bread alone, but on every word that comes from the mouth of God.' " *Matthew 4:4, quoting Deuteronomy 8:3*
"If you are the Son of God … throw yourself down [from the highest point of the Temple]." *Matthew 4:6*	"It is also written: 'Do not put the Lord your God to the test.' " *Matthew 4:7, quoting Deuteronomy 6:16*
"All [the kingdoms of the world] I will give you … if you will bow down and worship me." *Matthew 4:9*	"Away from me, Satan! For it is written: 'Worship the Lord your God, and serve him only.' *Matthew 4:10, quoting Deuteronomy 6:13*

Jesus quotes the two greatest commandments in the Old Testament

In Matthew 22:37-40, Jesus quotes from Deuteronomy 6:5:

"Love the Lord your God with all your heart and with all your soul and with all your mind."

In Matthew 22:39, Jesus quotes from Leviticus 19:18:

"Love your neighbor as yourself."

Jesus quotes from the Old Testament to explain his ministry

Jesus was in the synagogue of his home town, Nazareth, when he read from part of the Isaiah scroll (Isaiah 61:1-2).

"Jesus went to Nazareth, where he had been brought up, and on the Sabbath day he went into the synagogue, as was his custom. And he stood up to read. The scroll of the prophet Isaiah was handed to him. Unrolling it, he found the place where it is written:

'The Spirit of the Lord is on me, because he has anointed me to preach good news to the poor. He has sent me to proclaim freedom for the prisoners and recovery of sight for the blind, to release the oppressed, to proclaim the year of the Lord's favor.'

Then he rolled up the scroll, gave it back to the attendant and sat down. The eyes of everyone in the synagogue were fastened on him, and he began by saying to them, 'Today this scripture is fulfilled in your hearing.' "
Luke 4:16-21

Jesus predicts that his disciples will fall away

Jesus dramatically quotes Zechariah 13:7 in Matthew 26:31, to say that his followers will desert him:

"I will strike the shepherd, and the sheep of the flock will be scattered."

Jesus' words on the cross

As Jesus is dying, he quotes two highly significant passages from the Old Testament.

• Jesus quotes Psalm 22:1 after the three hours of darkness:

"Eloi, Eloi, lama sabachthani?" – which means, "My God, my God, why have you forsaken me?"
Matthew 27:46

• As Jesus prepares to say his final words, he calls out:

"I am thirsty." *John 19:28.*

Commenting on this, John writes:

"So that the Scripture would be fulfilled, Jesus said, 'I am thirsty.' "

Jesus was fulfilling the scriptures as he said these words. This is clear from Psalm 69:21:

"They … gave me vinegar for my thirst."

To ponder

• The risen Lord Jesus continued to use the Old Testament scriptures to explain his death and resurrection to his disciples. Read Luke 24:25-27. Also read Luke 24:45.

It's all Greek to me!

All 27 books of the New Testament are written in Greek. But you don't have to learn Greek to understand it, because there are so many excellent Bible translations. Just a little knowledge of Greek enhances our understanding of various passages and words.

Jesus on the cross

"It is finished," Jesus said from the cross. *John 19:30* In Greek, this is just one word of triumph: *"Tetelestai!"* It was a cry of victory, not a cry of despair.

Alpha and omega

Jesus is called the "alpha" and the "omega" three times in the Book of Revelation.

Alpha is the first letter of the Greek alphabet, and omega is the last. Jesus was saying that he is the beginning and end of everything.

"I am the alpha and the omega." *Revelation 1:8; 21:6; 22:13*

Eutheos!

Mark 1:12 reads, "At once the Spirit sent [Jesus] out into the desert."

The Greek word for "at once" is *eutheos*. It is used over forty times in Mark's Gospel – over half the occurrences in the whole of the New Testament. Its frequent usage reveals the dynamic pace of Mark's Gospel, as Jesus moves from one amazing act to another.

Dynamite!

Sometimes we become so familiar with our translation of the Bible that we forget the force of a particular word. In Romans 1:16, Paul talks about the power of the gospel. The Greek word for "power" is *dunamis*, from which we derive our word "dynamite." Paul is saying, "The gospel is dynamic or dynamite!"

Hypocrite

In the New Testament, the word "hypocrite" appears in the gospels of Matthew (thirteen times), Mark (one time), and Luke (three times). The word is used by Jesus only and it appears nowhere else in the New Testament.

"When you fast, do not look somber as the hypocrites do, for they display their faces to show men they are fasting."
Matthew 6:16

"Hypocrite" is simply the Greek word *hupokrites* written in English. It originally meant "actor." In Matthew 6:16, it is clear that the hypocrites were performing to an audience. The aim of this play-acting was to win human praise.

Love

Most Bibles translate the Greek words *philia* and *agape* by the word "love." *Philia* means brotherly love, the love we have for our family and friends. Paul writes to his Christian friends at Thessalonica, "Now about brotherly love we do not need to write to you."
1 Thessalonians 4:9

When the writers of the New Testament describe God's great love towards us, they want to make it clear that it is different and superior to the love humans have for each other. They use the word *agape*. John writes, "This is how God showed his love (*agape*) among us... God is love (*agape*)." *1 John 4:9, 16*

Something to do

• Consider learning New Testament Greek. That may sound difficult, but it is not impossible. Courses, some of which are correspondence courses, can teach you.

Finding God in every Old Testament book

Opening observations
• The Bible is a book about God.
• The Bible explains how God brings us his salvation.

From your reading of each Old Testament book, note one thing you discover about God (with a Bible reference).

The historical books of the Old Testament

Genesis 1:1	God is creator
Exodus 6:6	God is redeemer
Leviticus 20:7-8	God is holy
Numbers 14:22-23	God punishes those who reject him
Deuteronomy 10:12-13	What God requires of us
Joshua 1:8	God's recipe for success
Judges 2:20-21	God's warnings are clear
Ruth 4:17-22	God's plan for the redemption of the world
1 Samuel 15:22	God places great importance on obedience
2 Samuel 7:12-13	God's kingdom will last for ever
1 Kings 9:4-5	God requires integrity of heart
2 Kings 2:6	God is alive
1 Chronicles 29:11	The whole world belongs to God
2 Chronicles 16:9	God sees everything, especially those who are loyal to him
Ezra 1:1	God moves the hearts of rulers for his purposes
Nehemiah 6:15-16	God works through the efforts of godly people
Esther 4:14	God's special care for his people, revealing his will through things that happen. (Esther is the only Bible book in which God is not mentioned or directly referred to.)

"Yours, O Lord, is the greatness and the power
and the glory and the majesty and the splendor,
for everything in heaven and earth is yours.
Yours, O Lord, is the kingdom;
you are exalted as head over all."
1 Chronicles 29:11

Poetic books

Job 19:25	God our redeemer lives
Psalm 100:2	God is to be worshipped
Proverbs 1:7	We are to reverence God
Ecclesiastes 12:13-14	God will judge everything
Song of Solomon 8:7	God positively endorses marital love

"The fear of the Lord is the beginning of knowledge,
but fools despise wisdom and discipline."
Proverbs 1:7

Prophetic books

Isaiah 53:6	God has taken our sin upon himself
Jeremiah 31:33	God promises his new covenant
Lamentations 3:22-25	God is a God of mercy
Ezekiel 36:24-26	God promises to give us new hearts
Daniel 2:44	God rules over the nations
Hosea 14:4	God heals our turning away from him
Joel 2:28-29	The pouring out of the Holy Spirit is promised
Amos 5:12-14	God is against social injustice
Obadiah 21	God is to be king
Jonah 2:8-9	God brings salvation
Micah 6:8	God wants us to walk humbly before him
Nahum 1:7	God protects his followers
Habakkuk 3:17-19	God's strength is to be our strength
Zephaniah 3:15	God's presence is promised
Haggai 2:23	God chooses people to do his will
Zechariah 9:9	God appears in humility
Malachi 3:1	God is almighty

"I will heal their waywardness
and love them freely."
Hosea 14:4

Following a chain from Genesis to Revelation

Many key words in the Bible can be traced from Genesis to Revelation. The references which link up in this way are sometimes referred to as "chain" references.

The word "sin" – rebellion against God, and the concept of sinning against God, can be studied in this way.

Sin chain

Genesis 2:17	The fatal choice.
Genesis 13:13	Sin spreads.
Exodus 12:5-7	The blood of the killed lamb protects the people from death.
Exodus 32:7	The sin of making the golden calf.
Leviticus 16:6	Aaron makes a sin offering.
Numbers 14:18	The Lord forgives sin.
Numbers 32:23	Your sin will find you out.
Deuteronomy 20:18	Worshiping other gods is sin.
Joshua 22:17	Sin needs to be cleansed.
Judges 3:7	Forgetting God is sin.
1 Samuel 2:17	Showing contempt for God is sin.
2 Samuel 12:13	David confesses his sin.
1 Kings 15:26	Not being fully devoted to God is sin.
2 Kings 8:18	Doing evil in God's sight is sin.
1 Chronicles 9:1	Unfaithfulness to God is sin.
2 Chronicles 7:14	"If my people, who are called by my name, will humble themselves and pray and seek my face and turn from their wicked ways, then I will hear from heaven and forgive their sin and heal their land."
Ezra 6:17	As the Temple is dedicated, a sin offering is offered.
Nehemiah 1:6	Nehemiah identifies himself with the sin of Israel.
Job 1:5	Job shows his concern for any sins of his children.
Psalm 51:3	"My sin is always before me."
Proverbs 5:22	"The cords of his sin hold him fast."
Ecclesiastes 5:6	"Do not let your mouth lead you into sin."
Isaiah 6:5	"Woe is me … for I am a man of unclean lips, and I live among a people of unclean lips."
Jeremiah 14:7	Backsliding is sin.
Lamentations 1:5	Sin brings grief.

Ezekiel 18:4	"The soul who sins is the one who will die."
Daniel 4:27	"Renounce your sin by doing what is right."
Hosea 14:1	"Your sins have been your downfall."
Amos 5:12	"For I know how many are your offences and how great are your sins. You oppress the righteous and take bribes and you deprive the poor of justice in the courts."
Micah 6:7	Sin cannot be covered up by empty outward actions.
Zechariah 1:4	"Turn from your evil ways."
Matthew 5:27-28	Inward sins are not hidden from God.
Mark 7:20-23	Thirteen deadly sins.
Luke 18:11-14	The Pharisee and the tax-collector.
John 16:8-9	The Holy Spirit convicts us of sin.
Acts 2:36-41	God offers forgiveness for sin.
Romans 7:7-25	The "I" of self (sin) comes 32 times in Romans 7.
1 Corinthians 15:21	"Death came through a man."
Galatians 1:3-4	"The Lord Jesus Christ … gave himself for our sins."
Ephesians 1:7	"In him … we have forgiveness of sins."
Philippians 2:15	"A crooked and depraved generation …"
Colossians 2:11	"Putting off the sinful nature…"
1Thessalonians 2:16	"They always heap up their sins to the limit."
2 Thessalonians 2:12	Some people delight in wickedness.
1 Timothy 5:20	"Those who sin are to be rebuked publicly."
2 Timothy 3:6	"Loaded down with sins …"
Titus 3:11	Divisive people are "warped and sinful."
Hebrews 12:1	"Let us throw off … the sin which so easily entangles."
James 1:15	"Sin, when it is full grown, gives birth to death."
1 Peter 2:24	"He himself bore our sins in his body on the tree, so that we might die to sins and live for righteousness."
2 Peter 1:9	A reminder about being cleansed from sin.
1 John 1:7	"The blood of Jesus cleanses us from all sin."
Revelation 1:5	"… [He] has freed us from our sins."

Something to do

• Use a reference or chain reference Bible to do some more chain studies. Suggested topics: love, holiness, vine.

See also:
Looking through a microscope, page 14.
A year's worth of Bible studies, page 62.

The names of God

The names and titles given to God have special meanings. They tell us just how great he is.

Hebrew name	Meaning	Bible reference
Elohim	The All-Powerful One	*Genesis 1:1*
El (singular)	The Strong One	*Exodus 6:3*
El-Elyon	The Most High God	*Genesis 14:18-22*
El-Shaddai	The All-Sufficient One	*Genesis 17:1*
El-Olam	The Everlasting God	*Genesis 21:33*
Jehovah (Yahweh)	The Self-Existent One	*Exodus 3:14*
Jehovah-Elohim	Lord God, as Creator	*Genesis 1:26*
Jehovah-Jireh	Jehovah Will Provide	*Genesis 22:13-14*
Jehovah-Rapha	Jehovah Who Heals	*Exodus 15:25*
Jehovah-Nissi	Jehovah Is My Banner	*Exodus 17:15*
Jehovah-Shalom	Jehovah Is Peace	*Judges 6:24*
Jehovah-Shammah	Jehovah Is There	*Ezekiel 48:35*
Jehovah-Tsidkenu	Jehovah Our Righteousness	*Jeremiah 33:16*

Name in the Psalms	Meaning	Bible reference
Jehovah-Raah	The Lord Is My Shepherd	*Psalm 23:1*
Jehovah-Sabaoth	The Lord Of Hosts (God's power in time of trouble)	*Psalm 46:7*
The Living God	God gives strength	*Psalm 42:2*
King	God rules	*Psalm 44:4*
Strength	God gives us power	*Psalm 59:9*
Redeemer	The God who saves	*Psalm 78:35*
The One of Sinai	The God who gives the Law	*Psalm 68:8*

Other titles	Meaning	Bible reference
Rock	God's strength	*Deuteronomy 32:15*
Savior	God rescues	*Deuteronomy 32:15*
The Ancient of Days	God's global authority	*Daniel 7:9*
Father	God loves his family	*Ephesians 3:14*
God of gods, Lord of lords	The great, mighty God	*Deuteronomy 10:17*

Attributes	Example	Bible reference
God is compassionate	"compassionate and gracious"	*Exodus 34:6*
God is merciful	"his mercy is very great"	*1 Chronicles 21:13*
God is holy	"I am holy"	*Leviticus 11:44*
God is love	"God so loved the world"	*John 3:16*
God is Spirit	"God is Spirit"	*John 4:24*

Something to do
• Look up the above references to each name, title or attribute of God. Read the surrounding verses to understand more fully the significance of the name and why God was called by it.

Hopping about from book to book

Opening observation
One of the best ways of understanding the Bible is to compare one passage with another.

Genesis 1–3 and Revelation 20–22
The last three chapters of the Bible are understood more clearly in the light of the first three chapters of the Bible.

Read through Genesis 1–3 and Revelation 1–3. Work through the table on page 29, looking up the Bible references, then read the books again and see how your understanding has been increased.

Compare Revelation with Revelation
Sometimes one part of a Bible book sheds light on another part of the same book.

Read the descriptions of Jesus in chapters two and three of the Book of Revelation. You will find a short descriptive passage at the start of each of the seven letters. The verses to note are:

• Revelation 2:1	Seven stars…seven gold lampstands
• Revelation 2:8	The First and the Last
• Revelation 2:12	Sharp, double-edged sword
• Revelation 2:18	Eyes like blazing fire…feet like burnished bronze
• Revelation 3:1	Holding seven spirits of God and the seven stars
• Revelation 3:7	The keys of David
• Revelation 3:14	The Amen, the faithful and true witness

Now read the key to understanding these descriptions in Revelation 1:5–20, where John has his vision of Jesus. You will find that all the features described in chapters two and three refer to the picture of Jesus that John saw in chapter one.

Genesis chapters 1–3	Revelation chapters 20–22
In the beginning. *Genesis 1:1*	A new heaven and a new earth. *Revelation 21:1*
Darkness. *Genesis 1:5*	No night. *Revelation 21:25*
God made the sun and the moon. *Genesis 1:16*	No need for the sun or moon. *Revelation 21:23*
Death. *Genesis 2:17*	No more death. *Revelation 21:4*
Satan appears to deceive humankind. *Genesis 3:1*	Satan disappears forever. *Revelation 20:10*
A garden which become defiled. *Genesis 3:6-7*	A city with nothing shameful in it. *Revelation 21:27*
God's walk with us interrupted. *Genesis 3:8-10*	God's presence with us resumed. *Revelation 21:3*
The initial victory of the serpent. *Genesis 3:13*	The ultimate triumph of the Lamb. *Revelation 20:10; 22:3*
Sorrow is increased. *Genesis 3:16*	No more crying or pain. *Revelation 21:4*
The ground is cursed. *Genesis 3:17*	No longer will there be any curse. *Revelation 22:3*
The first paradise is closed. *Genesis 3:23*	The new paradise is opened. *Revelation 21:25*
Access to the tree of life is barred. *Genesis 3:24*	Access to the tree of life is reinstated. *Revelation 22:14*
They were driven out of the garden. *Genesis 3:24*	They will see his face. *Revelation 22:4*

Concluding thought

- Many of the symbols used in the Book of Revelation are explained in previous books of the Bible. You can see this as you look up the Bible references in the following table.

Symbol in Revelation	Reference in Revelation	Helpful Bible reference
Iron sceptre	*Revelation 2:27*	*Psalm 2:9*
Morning star	*Revelation 2:28*	*Daniel 12:3*
Key of David	*Revelation 3:7*	*Isaiah 22:22*
Lion, ox, man, eagle	*Revelation 4:7*	*Ezekiel 1:10; 10:14*
Lamb	*Revelation 5:8*	*John 1:29*

Study, if you dare, about God's wrath!

This is such a formidable and frightening subject that we are inclined to skip the study of God's wrath.

Who taught about heaven and hell?

It may come as a surprise to realize that the person who taught more about heaven and hell than anyone else, was Jesus himself.

Hell

It is hard to escape the conclusion that Jesus believed there was a counterpart to heaven, for those who were condemned before God.

The New Testament has a great deal of teaching on the subject of hell. It was Jesus who spoke about:

- People being in danger of "the fire of hell." *Matthew 5:22*
- A body to "be thrown into hell." *Matthew 5:29*
- The "soul and body [being destroyed] in hell." *Matthew 10:28*
- And who asked the Pharisees the question, "How will you escape being condemned to hell?" *Matthew 23:33*

God's wrath

- God's wrath is not to be confused with human anger or irritability.
- God is perfectly holy and righteous and can have nothing to do with evil.
- God's wrath is God's response to sin.
- People who refuse God's grace in Jesus are under God's wrath. *Romans 1:18; 2:5; Ephesians 2:3; Colossians 3:6*

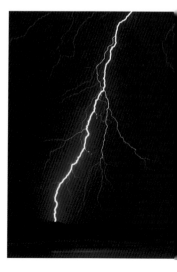

Descriptions of hell in the New Testament

Words used	Meaning	Bible references
Abaddon	Destruction	*Revelation 9:11*
Abyss	Valley of Hinnom. The rubbish dump outside Jerusalem. Child sacrifice by fire used to take place there. The place of final punishment in the New Testament.	*Matthew 5:22, 29-30* *Matthew 23:15-33* *Mark 9:43-47* *Luke 12:5* *James 3:6*
Hades	The place of the dead. From the name of the Greek god Hades. The word used in the New Testament for the Old Testament word *sheol*.	*Matthew 16:18* *Revelation 1:18; 6:8; 20:13; Matthew 11:23; Luke 10:15; Acts 2:27, 31; 1 Corinthians 15:55*
Lake of fire	John's symbol for "the second death."	*Revelation 19:20; 20:10, 14-15; 21:8*
Tartaros	Gloomy dungeon. In Greek mythology this was the place of eternal punishment.	*2 Peter 2:4*

An illustration of God's wrath

A good example of God's wrath in action is Jesus' reaction to the traders in the Temple, described by John:

When it was almost time for the Jewish Passover, Jesus went up to Jerusalem. In the Temple courts he found men selling cattle, sheep and doves, and others sitting at tables exchanging money.
So he made a whip out of cords, and drove all from the Temple area, both sheep and cattle; he scattered the coins of the money changers and overturned their tables. To those who sold doves he said, "Get these out of here! How dare you turn my Father's house into a market!"

His disciples remembered that it is written, "Zeal for your house will consume me."
John 2:13-17

Hundreds of years of Bible history in 20 verses

The long history books of the Old Testament may seem incomprehensible. One way to approach them is to read summaries.

Stephen's summary

Before Stephen was stoned, he summarized God's actions in the history of God's people.

Read the speech Stephen made before the Sanhedrin, and then read the fuller account from the Old Testament references.

(2) Brothers and fathers, listen to me! The God of glory appeared to our father Abraham while he was still in Mesopotamia, before he lived in Haran. (3) "Leave your country and your people," God said, "and go to the land I will show you."

(4) So he left the land of the Chaldeans and settled in Haran. After the death of his father, God sent him to this land where you are now living. (5) He gave him no inheritance here, not even a foot of ground. But God promised him that he and his descendants after him would possess the land, even though at that time Abraham had no child. (6) God spoke to him in this way: "Your descendants will be strangers in a country not their own, and they will be enslaved and ill-treated for four hundred years. (7) But I will punish the nation they serve as slaves," God said, "and afterwards they will come out of that country and worship me in this place."

(8) Then he gave Abraham the covenant of circumcision. And Abraham became the father of Isaac and circumcised him eight days after his birth. Later Isaac became the father of Jacob, and Jacob became the father of the twelve patriarchs.

(9) Because the patriarchs were jealous of Joseph, they sold him as a slave into Egypt. But God was with him (10) and rescued him from all his troubles. He gave Joseph wisdom and enabled him to gain the goodwill of Pharaoh king of Egypt; so he made him ruler over Egypt and all his palace.

(11) Then a famine struck all Egypt and Canaan, bringing great suffering, and our fathers could not find food. (12) When Jacob heard that there was grain in Egypt, he sent our fathers on their first visit. (13) On their second visit, Joseph told his brothers who he was, and Pharaoh learned about Joseph's family. (14) After this, Joseph sent for his father

Jacob and his whole family, seventy-five in all. (15) Then Jacob went down to Egypt, where he and our fathers died. (16) Their bodies were brought back to Shechem and placed in the tomb that Abraham had bought from the sons of Hamor at Shechem for a certain sum of money.

(17) As the time drew near for God to fulfil his promise to Abraham, the number of our people in Egypt greatly increased. (18) Then another king, who knew nothing about Joseph, became ruler of Egypt. (19) He dealt treacherously with our people and oppressed our forefathers by forcing them to throw out their newborn babies so that they would die.

(20) At that time Moses was born, and he was no ordinary child. For three months he was cared for in his father's house. (21) When he was placed outside, Pharaoh's daughter took him and brought him up as her own son.
Acts 7:2-21

Stephen's speech – Old Testament references

Acts 7:2-8. The experience of Abraham
Acts 7:2   Read with Genesis 11:31; 15:7.
Acts 7:3   Read with Genesis 12:1.
Acts 7:4   Read with Genesis 12:5.
Acts 7:5   Read with Genesis 12:7; 17:8; 26:3.
Acts 7:6   Read with Exodus 1:8-11; 12:40.
Acts 7:7   Read with Genesis 15:13-14; Exodus 3:12.
Acts 7:8   Read with Genesis 17:9-14; 21:2-4; 25:26; 29:31-35; 30:5-13, 17-24; 35:16-18, 22-26.

Acts 7:9-16. The experience of Joseph
Acts 7:9a   Read with Genesis 37:4, 11.
Acts 7:9b   Read with Genesis 37:28; Psalm 105:17.
Acts 7:9c   Read with Genesis 39:2, 21, 23; Haggai 2:4.
Acts 7:10   Read with Genesis 41:37-43; Psalm 105:20-22.
Acts 7:11   Read with Genesis 41:54.
Acts 7:12   Read with Genesis 42:1-2.
Acts 7:13   Read with Genesis 45:1-4; 45:16.
Acts 7:14   Read with Genesis 45:9-10; 46:26-27; Exodus 1:5; Deuteronomy 10:22.
Acts 7:15   Read with Genesis 46:5-7; 49:33; Exodus 1:6.
Acts 7:16   Read with Genesis 23:16-20; 33:18-19; 50:13; Joshua 24:32.

Acts 7:17-21. The experience of Moses
Acts 7:17   Read with Exodus 1:7; Psalm 105:24.
Acts 7:18   Read with Exodus 1:8.
Acts 7:19   Read with Exodus 1:10-22.
Acts 7:20   Read with Exodus 2:2.
Acts 7:21   Read with Exodus 2:3-10.

A biography - the life of Daniel

Opening observations
Nothing bad or negative is recorded about Daniel.
This is in striking contrast to people such as:
- David (a liar, adulterer and murderer).
- Jonah (who deliberately disobeyed God).
- Elijah (who expressed the wish to commit suicide).

Build up a picture about Daniel's circumstances
Find out about Daniel's background:
- Daniel was a prisoner of war. *Daniel 1:1-2*
- Daniel's family. *Daniel 1:3*
- The seven things mentioned about him. *Daniel 1:5*
- The gifts God gave him. *Daniel 1:17*

Compile a character profile of Daniel
- He shares problems with his friends. *Daniel 2:17*
- He takes his problems to God in prayer. *Daniel 2:18*
- He remembers to thank God for answered prayer. *Daniel 2:19-23*
- He makes it clear that his gifts are given him by God. *Daniel 2:27-28*
- He does not let honors go to his head. *Daniel 2:48-49; 5:29*
- He tells the truth, even if it means he might suffer for speaking up. *Daniel 5:1-31*
- He trusts God, even if it means he might be killed. *Daniel 6*

Daniel in the lions' den
Read chapter six, no matter how well you know the story. Note the following points.
- Even the best of God's followers are persecuted: see what Daniel was accused of. *Verses 1-9*
- Daniel deliberately goes against the king's decree. Why? *Verses 10-12*
- Daniel's faithfulness has quite an effect on the king. *Verses 13-18*
- How does Daniel give God the glory for what happened? *Verses 19-23*

Daniel's friends
Study chapter three, where Daniel's friends are thrown into the fiery furnace. In what ways do the men show their faith in God?

Concluding thought
- Daniel was about eighty years old when he was put in the
  lions' den. But he stayed faithful to God in his old age:
  "My God sent his angel, and he shut the mouths of the lions."
  Daniel 6:22

Making study a spiritual exercise

We read and study the Bible primarily for our spiritual lives.
A good prayer before reading the Bible is:

Lord Jesus Christ,
May I love you more dearly,
Follow you more nearly,
See you more clearly,
Day by day. Amen.

Making comparisons

See how many links you can make between Isaiah 53 and what you know about Jesus' death.

Making a spiritual response

To prevent Bible study from being little more than an intellectual exercise, remember this, as you think about Jesus' death: "All this you have done for me, what will I do for you?"

Something to do

· Memorize Isaiah 53.
· Try learning one verse a day, or one a week. Repeat it to yourself during the day, and before you go to sleep.

See also:

· *15 ways to enhance your Bible study*, page 64.

Who has believed our message
and to whom has the arm of the
Lord been revealed?
He grew up before him like a
tender shoot,
and like a root out of dry ground.
He had no beauty or majesty to
attract us to him,
nothing in his appearance that we
should desire him.
He was despised and rejected by
men, a man of sorrows, and
familiar with suffering.
Like one from whom men hide
their faces
he was despised, and we esteemed
him not.
Surely he took up our infirmities
and carried our sorrows,
yet we considered him stricken by
God,
smitten by him, and afflicted.
But he was pierced for our
transgressions,
he was crushed for our iniquities;
the punishment that brought us
peace was upon him,
and by his wounds we are healed.

We all, like sheep, have gone
  astray,
each of us has turned to his own
  way;
and the Lord has laid on him
the iniquity of us all.
He was oppressed and afflicted
yet he did not open his mouth;
he was led like a lamb to the
  slaughter,
and as a sheep before her shearers
  is silent,
so he did not open his mouth.
By oppression and judgment he
  was taken away.
And who can speak of his
  descendants?
For he was cut off from the land
  of the living;
for the transgression of my people
  he was stricken.
He was assigned a grave with the
  wicked,
and with the rich in his death,
though he had done no violence,
nor was any deceit in his mouth.

Yet it was the Lord's will to crush
  him and cause him to suffer,
and though the Lord makes his
  life a guilt offering,
he will see his offspring and
  prolong his days,
and the will of the Lord will
  prosper in his hand.
After the suffering of his soul,
he will see the light of life and be
  satisfied;
by his knowledge my righteous
  servant will justify many,
and he will bear their iniquities.
Therefore I will give him a portion
  among the great,
and he will divide the spoils with
  the strong,
because he poured out his life
  unto death,
and was numbered with the
  transgressors.
For he bore the sin of many,
and made intercession for the
  transgressors.

Isaiah 53

Three men with a common desire – a death wish

Elijah, Jonah and Job all expressed the desire to die before their lives naturally ended. They are among some of God's greatest, strongest, and most faithful followers who at times felt like committing suicide.

ELIJAH the discouraged prophet

Elijah's death-wish

"Elijah was afraid and ran for his life. When he came to Beersheba in Judah, he left his servant there, while he himself went a day's journey into the desert. He came to a broom tree, sat down under it and prayed that he might die. 'I have had enough, Lord,' he said. 'Take my life; I am no better than my anscestors.' " *1 Kings 19:3-4*

• Read *1 Kings 19:5-9* to see how God comforted Elijah.

A bird's-eye view of Elijah's life

• He predicts famine in Israel. *1 Kings 17:1*
• He is fed by ravens. *1 Kings 17:2-6*
• He defeats the prophets of Baal. *1 Kings 18:16-46*
• He is taken to heaven in a whirlwind. *2 Kings 2:11-12*

JONAH – the man who wanted to avoid doing God's will

Jonah's death-wish

"When the sun rose, God provided a scorching east wind, and the sun blazed on Jonah's head so that he grew faint. He wanted to die, and said, 'It would be better for me to die than to live.' "
Jonah 4:8

- Read *Jonah 4:9-11* to see how God helped Jonah.

A bird's-eye view of Jonah's life

- He tries to run away from God. *Jonah 1*
- He prays inside a fish. *Jonah 2*
- He preaches to Nineveh. *Jonah 3*
- He is rebuked by God. *Jonah 4*

JOB – the man who suffered

Job's death-wish

"After this, Job opened his mouth and cursed the day of his birth. He said: 'Why did I not perish at birth, and die as I came from the womb?' "
Job 3:1-2, 11

- Read *Job 40:1-42:3* to see how God brought Job to worship him.

A bird's-eye view of Job's life

- His righteousness is tested by disaster. *Job 1*
- He keeps on saying that he is innocent. *Job 3-41*
- He worships God and is restored. *Job 42*

To ponder
- "Carry each other's burdens." *Galatians 6:2*

What's so fishy about Jonah?

Opening observations

People who describe the fish as a whale are incorrect. The correct translation is "great fish" or "large fish" (*Jonah 1:17*). Jesus calls it a "huge fish" (*Matthew 12:40*). The biological identification of the fish is not the important point of the story.

Read through the four chapters of Jonah

As you do this, bear in mind that the whole story hinges on Jonah's refusal to obey God, and his reluctant decision to go to the wicked town of Nineveh and speak out against it.

- **Chapter 1.** As you read chapter one, reflect on how the Lord saves pagan sailors from drowning at sea.

- **Chapter 2.** As you read chapter two, reflect on how the Lord also saves Jonah from drowning.

- **Chapter 3.** As you read chapter three, reflect on how the Lord saves the people of Nineveh from judgment.

- **Chapter 4.** As you read chapter four, reflect on how the Lord saves Jonah from his wrong ideas.

Questions to ask

What do we learn about Jonah?

- He runs away from God – at least he does his level best to! *Jonah 1:3, 10.* (Tarshish was in the opposite direction to Nineveh. Imagine Jonah was in London, and God told him to travel to New York, but he boarded the plane for Beijing, China.)
- When God is merciful, Jonah is angry. *Jonah 4:1-3, 9.* (Jonah was more concerned about a plant than about the people. *Read Jonah 4:10-11.*)
- Jonah prays to God. *Jonah 1:9; 2:1-9*

What do we learn about God?

- Throughout the Book of Jonah, it is assumed that God is fair and just and that he will punish wrong. *Jonah 1:2; 3:2, 9-10*
- God is in control of his world, which includes the weather, animals and plants. The great fish was God's way of rescuing Jonah. *Jonah 1:4, 9, 17; 2:10; 4:6-8*
- God shows how merciful and kind he is – to animals as well as to humans. *Jonah 2:8-9; 3:9-10; 4:2, 10-11*

Concluding thought

- What spiritual lesson did Jesus draw from Jonah? *Read Matthew 12:38-41; 16:4.* (Jonah, God's servant, was miraculously rescued by God. In the same way, Jesus' claims will be seen to be true through his resurrection. *Read Romans 1:3-4.*)

The great women of the Bible

Opening observations

Jesus surprised people by the way he cared for, talked to, and respected women.

John's Gospel says that Jesus' disciples were once "greatly surprised" to find Jesus talking to a woman, for religious teachers did not speak to women in public in those days. *John 4:27*

Look up the Bible references given for each woman. Write down her good points.

Ten great women of the Old Testament

Deborah	The only judge (ruler) who gave Israel twenty years of peace.	*Judges 4-5*
Eve	The first woman.	*Genesis 2:18-4:2; 4:25*
Esther	Heroine of the Book of Esther.	*Esther*
Miriam	Moses' sister.	*Exodus 2:4, 7-8; 15:20-21; Numbers 12; 20:1*
Naomi	Ruth's mother-in-law.	*Ruth*
Rachel	Laban's daughter.	*Genesis 29-30; 35:18-20*
Rahab	Prostitute who lived in Jericho.	*Joshua 2; 6:22-25; Matthew 1:5; James 2:25*
Rebekah	Isaac's wife.	*Genesis 24; 25:19-26:16, 27*
Ruth	Heroine of the Book of Ruth.	*Ruth*
Sarah	Abraham's wife.	*Genesis 11-12; 16-18:15; 20-21*

Seven great women of the New Testament

Anna	An old prophetess, who practically lived in the Temple.	*Luke 2:36-38*
Dorcas (also called Tabitha)	Dorcas was renowned for caring for the poor.	*Acts 9:36-41*
Elizabeth	Related to Mary, the mother of Jesus.	*Luke 1*
Lydia	A successful businesswoman who became a follower of Jesus.	*Acts 16:14-15, 40*
Martha and Mary	Sisters of Lazarus.	*Luke 10:38-42; John 11, 12:1-9*
Mary	The mother of Jesus.	*Matthew 1:18-25; 2:11; 13:55; Luke 1-2; John 2:1-11; 19:25-27; Acts 1:14*

Mary's song

My soul praises the Lord
and my spirit rejoices in God my Savior;
for he has been mindful
of the humble estate of his servant.
From now on all generations will call me blessed,
for the Mighty One has done great things for me –
holy is his name.
His mercy extends to those who fear him,
from generation to generation.
He has performed mighty deeds with his arm;
he has scattered those who are proud in their inmost thoughts.
He has brought down rulers from their
    thrones
but has lifted up the humble.
He has filled the hungry with good things
but he has sent the rich away empty.
He has helped his servant Israel,
remembering to be merciful
to Abraham and his descendants for ever,
even as he said to our fathers.
Luke 1:46-55

Concluding thought
• In an age when women were despised and marginalized, the apostle Paul's statement in Galatians 3:28 was revolutionary.

Coming to grips with the Bible's longest chapter

Opening observation

The 176 verses of Psalm 119 make it, by far, the longest chapter in the Bible.

Working out the theme of Psalm 119 is not hard

Psalm 119 is about God's revelation to Israel. Nearly all of its 176 verses refer to the same thing. They focus on God's words and his law (verse 160) as statements about what to believe (doctrine) and how to behave (ethics).

Eight synonyms

The poetic writer of Psalm 119 uses eight words to celebrate God's revelation. You'll find one of the following words in just about every verse:

1 Precepts (verse 4).
2 Law ("the law of the Lord" verse 1).
3 Statutes (verse 24).
4 Decrees (verse 5).
5 Commands (verse 6).
6 Word or words (verse 17).
7 Laws (verse 13).
8 Promises (verse 41).

There is another word which also comes up often: "ways" (verse 3). This means a pattern of life based on God's will.

Eight definitions

As you read through this hymn of praise to God's revelation, match these definitions to the above eight synonyms.

1 Detailed rules for life.
2 Divinely revealed teaching.
3 Details about God's covenant which his people are to observe.
4 Written down rulings which are always to be observed.
5 A word that expresses the will of a personal God, who is Israel's Lord.
6 Communication of God's will to his people.
7 Verdicts of the divine judge about a wide range of topics.
8 Communication of God's will, specifically through his promises.

Breaking down 176 verses

If we could read the Hebrew language and had a Hebrew Bible, the pattern behind these 176 verses would be obvious. But English Bibles give clues to the pattern:

- Notice how many verses each section is split into.
- Count the number of sections in these 176 verses.

Working out the pattern

- The number of sections is the same as the number of letters in the Hebrew alphabet.

  22 sections x 8 verses = 176 verses.

- The whole of Psalm 119 is one long alphabetic acrostic.

  In Hebrew, the first letter of each verse in the first section, is the first letter of the Hebrew alphabet.

  The first letter in each verse in the second section is the second letter of the Hebrew alphabet, and so on, through to the last letter of the Hebrew alphabet in section 22.

- Some Bibles have the headings to indicate this. Before verses 1-8 is the word "Aleph," before verses 9-16 is the word "Beth," and so on.

Concluding thought

See how much the writer valued God's revelation (verses 103, 14, 72, 127, 47, 70, 111, 174, 20, 40, 171-172).

Something to do

- Compose your own acrostic psalm, using the English alphabet, in honor of God's word.

The names and titles of Jesus

The name "Jesus" is the Greek form of the word "Joshua," meaning "Yahweh is salvation." This is made clear in Matthew 1:21: "You are to give him the name Jesus, because he will save his people from their sins."

Titles used for Jesus in the Old Testament

There are six names which refer to Jesus in the Book of Isaiah.
• Immanuel, God with us. *Isaiah 7:14*
• Wonderful Counselor, Mighty God, Everlasting Father, Prince of Peace. *Isaiah 9:6*
• Root of Jesse. *Isaiah 11:10*
• Branch. *Zechariah 6:12*

Titles used for Jesus in the gospels

Every title, or name used to refer to Jesus, reveals his character.

Title used	Significance	Bible reference
Teacher/Rabbi and **The Teacher**	Jesus taught people about God	*Mark 5:35*
Prophet	He spoke the word of God	*Luke 24:19*
Christ (Greek for Anointed One/Messiah.)	Sent to establish God's kingdom on earth	*John 1:41*
I Am	Jesus existed before his human life on earth	*John 8:58*
The Lamb of God	Jesus would be a sacrifice for sin	*John 1:29*
Jesus the Nazarene	To distinguish him from other people called Jesus	*Matthew 2:23*
Son of David	Descended from David. Fulfilled all the promises made to King David.	*Matthew 15:22*
Son of God	Jesus was uniquely related to God	*Mark 1:1*
Son of Man	Showing his human identity	*Matthew 8:20*
Word	How Jesus revealed God	*John 1:1*
Rabboni	My dear Master	*John 20:16*
Lord	A title showing respect	*Luke 11:1*

Titles for Jesus in the rest of the New Testament

Title	Significance	Bible reference
Alpha and Omega	The beginning and the end	*Revelation 1:8*
Author of life	The one who gives life	*Acts 3:15*
The bright Morning Star	The one who brings light	*Revelation 22:16*
Head of the Church	The overseer of all Christians	*Ephesians 5:23*
Holy and Righteous One	Jesus was both holy and righteous	*Acts 3:14*
King of kings and Lord of lords	Ruler of all	*Revelation 19:16*
Lamb	Lamb killed as a sacrifice for sin	*Revelation 5:6-13*
Lion of the tribe of Judah	A title of the Messiah from the family of David	*Revelation 5:5*
Root of David	A title of the Messiah from the family of David	*Revelation 5:5*
Savior	One who saves from sin	*1 John 4:14*
Word of God	Gives voice to God's truth	*Revelation 19:13*

- In the seven "I ams" described in John's Gospel, Jesus uses seven figurative descriptions of himself. See: *What's so special about John's Gospel?* page 54.

Studying the life of Jesus

Opening observations
• Nearly everything we know about Jesus comes from the four gospels: Matthew, Mark, Luke and John.
• Many people have strong views about Jesus, but few people have taken the time to read the gospels.

Twelve highlights of Jesus' life
Questions to ask as you read through the highlights
• Why do you think the writer included this particular story in his gospel?
• What does this event tell us about who Jesus was?

1	His birth	*Luke 2:1-7*
2	The visit of the shepherds	*Luke 2:8-20*
3	The wise men and their gifts	*Matthew 2:1-12*
4	The twelve-year-old Jesus visits the Temple	*Luke 2:41-50*
5	Jesus' baptism	*Matthew 3:13-17*
6	Jesus is tempted	*Matthew 4:1-11*
7	A top religious leader talks to Jesus	*John 3:1-21*
8	Jesus speaks to a despised female half-caste	*John 4:1-42*
9	Jesus chooses his team	*Matthew 10:1-4*
10	Peter gets it right	*Matthew 16:13-20*
11	The transfiguration of Jesus	*Matthew 17:1-13*
12	The ascension of Jesus	*Luke 24:50-53*

Getting to know and to love the gospels
Here is a simple way to read through the gospels in less than thirteen weeks.
• Read a chapter a day of Mark's Gospel (16 days).
• Read a chapter a day of Matthew's Gospel (28 days).
• Read a chapter a day of Luke's Gospel (24 days).
• Read a chapter a day of John's Gospel (21 days).

It's a fact
The shortest verse in the Bible is John 11:35. It has two words, one in Greek.

What did Jesus say?

Occasion	Bible reference	Theme
Sermon on the Mount	*Matthew 5-7*	The way to be happy
The upper room	*John 13-17*	How to live the Jesus way
The Mount of Olives	*Matthew 24-25*	The shape of the future

What did Jesus do?

Miracle	Bible reference	Spiritual truth demonstrated
Paralytic healed	*Luke 5*	The forgiveness of sins
5,000 people fed	*John 6*	Jesus is the bread of life
Various miracles	*Matthew 8*	Jesus' authority over disease

How did people respond to Jesus?

People	Response	Reasons
Leaders	Few believed	They rejected Jesus because: • He said he was God. *John 5:18* • They disapproved of the company he kept. *Mark 2:16* • He challenged their traditions. *Mark 7:1-13*
Crowds	Many believed	Examples of those who welcomed Jesus: • Many Samaritans. *John 4:39* • Many Jews. *John 11:45* • Crowds listened to Jesus with delight. *Mark 12:37* • People rejected by society. *Luke 15:1*

Concluding thought
• As you read the four gospels, compile your own biography of Jesus. Use the four headings on this page, and write down what happened, with its reference in the gospels.

See also: *A year's worth of Bible studies*, page 62.

How do Matthew, Mark and Luke differ?

In one sense, the four gospels are similar, as they are all portraits of the life, death and resurrection of Jesus. But each gospel also contains a special message. One way to unlock the special message is to work out what is different about each gospel.

Matthew's Gospel

Jesus' words
Two-thirds of Matthew's Gospel, 1,071 verses, records the spoken words of Jesus.

Jesus is king
Matthew presents Jesus as Israel's promised messianic king. Look up the following Bible references, which clearly reveal a portrait of Jesus as a ruler or king. *1:23; 2:2; 2:6; 3:17; 4:15-17; 21:5; 21:9; 22:44-45; 26:64; 27:11; 27:27-37*

Mark's Gospel

Mark's message
It's not too hard to see what Mark's main message is. From reading Mark 1:1, it is clear that this gospel is all about Jesus, the Son of God.

The humanity of Jesus
Mark emphasizes the humanity and kindness of Jesus.
• Jesus is "deeply distressed." *3:5*
• Jesus has "compassion" for a large crowd. *6:34*

Luke's Gospel

Luke was a Gentile, not a Jew. He wrote his gospel for the Gentiles. Luke took great pains to stress that Jesus was for everyone, not just the Jews.
In his gospel, Luke presents Jesus as the savior of the world, and shows that Jesus came:
• For women as well as men.
• For slaves as well as for free men.
• For the poor as well as for the rich.
• For people who had not been brought up as Jews.

Father God

Matthew's favorite way of describing God is to refer to him as "heavenly Father" or "Father in heaven." What do we learn from the following verses about God our Father? *5:16; 5:45; 5:48; 6:1; 6:9; 7:11; 7:21; 10:32-3; 12:50; 16:17; 18:10; 18:14; 18:19*

A gospel for Jews

Matthew quotes from the Old Testament more often than the other three gospels.

- Matthew shows his Jewish readers, through these quotes, that Jesus really was the Messiah prophesied in the Old Testament.
- Matthew indicates that Jesus came from the Jews.
- Matthew demonstrates that many events in Jesus' life – birth, early childhood, teachings, miracles, arrest, death and resurrection – fulfilled prophesies about him written hundreds of years before in the Old Testament.

- Jesus is deeply distressed and "troubled." *14:33*
- The gospel's favorite title for Jesus is "Son of Man," used fourteen times. This title appears in Daniel 7:13-14, where it is used of the Messiah. It is a title that is never used by anyone but Jesus. *10:45*

Jesus is the Son of God

Mark shows how Jesus is the Son of God.
- Read about the many times Mark refers to Jesus as the "Son of God." *1:1, 11; 3:11; 9:7; 12:6; 13:32; 14:36, 61*
- Mark shows that Jesus acted with divine authority. In his conflicts with the Pharisees, Jesus acts and speaks as God. *2:1-12, 15-17, 18-22, 23-38; 3:1-6*

Discipleship

Mark concentrates on the death of Jesus on the cross, and the need for Jesus' disciples to follow him in a life of self-renunciation. *8:34-9:1; 9:35-10:31; 10:42-45*

Key themes in Luke

There are six themes to look for. List the themes, and write down the related Bible references, as you come across them.
- **Prayer**
- **Money**
- **The Holy Spirit**
- **Forgiveness**
- **Praise and joy**
- **Women and children**

Incidents recorded only by Luke

Many events only appear in Luke's Gospel. See how they fit in with the six key themes mentioned above.
- Zechariah's vision and Elizabeth's conception. *1:5-25*
- Gabriel's visit to Mary. *1:26-38*
- Mary's visit to Elizabeth. *1:39-56*
- Birth of John the Baptist and Zechariah's song. *1:57-80*
- The decree of Caesar Augustus. *2:1-3*
- Jesus' birth in Bethlehem. *2:4-7*
- The shepherds. *2:8-20*
- Jesus' circumcision. *2:21*
- Jesus is presented in the Temple; Simeon and Anna. *2:22-40*

Choose a topic and make a Bible study

Profitable Bible studies can been made by studying words, themes, teachings, people and events in the Bible. You will need a Bible concordance or Bible dictionary to examine the places where your specific topic of study is found.

Baptism

Let's see if we can discover some of the meanings for this rather controversial subject. The word "baptism" or "baptize" is an interesting word to study because the word was never translated into English from the Greek *baptisma* or *baptizo*. To stay away from current controversies surrounding baptism, the translators left the word untranslated.

The best approach for discovering the meaning of baptism, is to look at all the Bible verses where this word occurs.

John the Baptist

The first occurrence of the word and its variations is in Matthew chapter three.

• Why was John called John the Baptist?	Because he was baptizing people. *Matthew 3:6*
• What substance did John use for baptism?	Water in the River Jordan. *Matthew 3:6, 11, 13*
• What did the people normally do prior to baptism?	They confessed their sins. *Matthew 3:6*
• Why did John baptize at a certain area in the River Jordan?	Because there was plenty of water there. *John 3:23*

Summarize what you have learned so far about baptism.

Jesus' baptism

• Where was Jesus baptized?	In the River Jordan: he went up out of the water. *Matthew 3:13, 16*
• Why was Jesus baptized?	To fulfill all righteousness. *Matthew 3:14-15*
• What were the last words of Jesus before he ascended to heaven?	To go and make disciples of all nations, baptizing them into the name of the Father, Son and Holy Spirit. *Matthew 28:19-20*

Baptism in Acts

In Acts chapter two, we find the first occurrence of baptism as the Church begins on the Day of Pentecost. If you look up each of the following passages from Acts, you will discover that a believer in Christ always submitted immediately to baptism.

Acts 2:38-41   *Acts 9:17-18*   *Acts 16:31-33*
Acts 8:12-13   *Acts 10:47-48*   *Acts 19:3-5*
Acts 8:36, 38   *Acts 16:14-15*   *Acts 22:16*

Finding out about baptism

Romans 6:3-5   *1 Corinthians 12:13*   *Ephesians 4:5*
1 Corinthians 1:13-16 *Galatians 3:27*   *Colossians 2:12*

In other passages throughout the New Testament, the term "baptism" also occurs. As you look up these passages, see if you can determine more fully the meaning and the importance of baptism.

There are some preliminary observations that we can make as we assemble all the information about baptism.

• It involves water (probably much).
• It involves confession of sin.
• It is important – it is something that God wants us to submit to.
• It was important enough for Jesus to submit to.

• As believers, we are told to baptize the disciples we make.
• It is the one thing in the Christian life that we are told to do only once.
• It involves us in a unique relationship with Jesus.

Concluding thought

• So now it is up to you to study and make up your own mind as to what baptism means to you. Look up each verse. Jot down some notes. Then come to your own conclusions.

What's so special about John's Gospel?

Opening observations

Matthew, Mark and Luke are similar to each other, but John is quite different.

Many of the incidents mentioned in John's Gospel, such as Jesus' washing of the disciples' feet (John 13:1-17), are not in Matthew, Mark or Luke.

Signs

One distinctive characteristic of John's Gospel is the fact that he does not talk about miracles, but signs.

Start by reading John 20:31, as John states why he recorded these miraculous signs. As you look up each sign, consider how it helped to reinforce who Jesus was.

The seven signs

1	Jesus changes water into wine	*John 2:1-10*
2	Jesus heals a royal official's son	*John 4:46-54*
3	Jesus heals an invalid	*John 5:1-9*
4	Jesus feeds 5,000	*John 6:1-14*
5	Jesus walks on the water	*John 6:16-21*
6	Jesus heals a blind man	*John 9:1-41*
7	Jesus brings Lazarus back to life	*John 11:1-44*

"I am"

John loved the number seven. As well as recording seven miraculous signs, he lists the seven "I am" sayings of Jesus.

The seven "I am" sayings

"I am the bread of life"	*John 6:35-40*
"I am the light of the world"	*John 8:12-13*
"I am the gate"	*John 10:7-10*
"I am the good shepherd"	*John 10:11-18*
"I am the resurrection and the life"	*John 11:17-27*
"I am the way, truth and life"	*John 14:1-7*
"I am the true vine"	*John 15:1-11*

Links

Did you know that some of the signs link up with the "I ams"? For example, the seventh sign links with the fifth "I am." You can link up others as well. Link the first sign and the seventh "I am," the fourth sign and the first "I am," the sixth sign and the second "I am."

Concluding thought

• In his gospel, John used a thematic approach rather than the chronological approach favored by Matthew, Mark and Luke.

• See how many of the following key word concepts you can find as you read John's Gospel: truth, light, darkness, word, knowledge, remain, love, world, judgment, belief and witness.

Studying a single word: humility

For a good Bible definition of humility, see Romans 12:3. Another word for humility could be honesty.

One of the most famous Old Testament figures is called a humble person (in fact he was called "a very humble" man)	*Numbers 12:3*
Humility is not false modesty	*Colossians 2:23.*
Humility is linked to receiving God's salvation	*Psalm 149:4*
Humility is linked to receiving grace from God	*Proverbs 3:34*
In the Bible we are commanded to be humble	*Micah 6:8*
Humility is commended by Jesus	*Matthew 18:4*
Humility brings rewards	*Proverbs 15:33; 1 Peter 5:6.*
• The humble person is guided by God	*Psalm 25:9*
• The humble person enjoys God's help	*James 4:6*
• The humble person is promised rest of heart and mind	*Matthew 11:28-30*
• The humble person will be lifted up	*Matthew 23:12*
Humility is one of God's characteristics	
• God's humility is seen in his creation of and care for the world	*Psalm 113:5-9*
• God's humility is seen in his being prepared to live with lowly people	*Isaiah 57:15*
• God's humility is seen in his lowly birth in a manger	*Luke 1:32-35*
• God's humility is seen in his death	*Philippians 2:5-8*
Humility was one of Jesus' most obvious qualities	*Matthew 11:29 and John 8:50.*

Learning from Jesus' humility.   *2 Corinthians 10:1*
When the apostle Paul wanted to emphasize
the lesson about humility, he appealed to
Jesus' own humility

Humility is linked with
- Wisdom   *James 3:13*
- Compassion, kindness, gentleness
  and patience   *Colossians 3:12*
- Righteousness   *Zephaniah 2:3*

Concluding thought
- We are expected to get dressed each day in a set of humble
  clothes, according to 1 Peter 5:5.

The death of Jesus

Opening observation

The four gospel writers give more space to Jesus' death than to any other event in his life.

The order of the events linked to Jesus' crucifixion

1	Arrival at Golgotha (Calvary)	*Matthew 27:33; Mark 15:22; Luke 23:33; John 19:7*
2	Offer of a numbing drink	*Matthew 27:34*
3	The crucifixion	*Matthew 27:35*
4	"Father forgive ..." (First "word" from the cross)	*Luke 23:34*
5	Gambling for Jesus' clothes	*Matthew 27:35*
6	Jesus is mocked.	*Matthew 27:39-44; Mark 15:29*
7	The thieves speak against Jesus, but one believes	*Matthew 27:44*
8	"Today you will be with me ..." (Second "word" from the cross)	*Luke 23:43*
9	"Dear woman, here is your son ..." (Third "word" from the cross)	*John 19:26-27*
10	The darkness	*Matthew 27:45; Mark 15:33*
11	"My God, my God ..." (Fourth "word" from the cross)	*Matthew 27:46-47; Mark 15:34-36*
12	"I am thirsty." (Fifth "word" from the cross)	*John 19:28*
13	"It is finished." (Sixth "word" from the cross)	*John 19:30*
14	"Father, into your hands ..." (Seventh "word" from the cross)	*Luke 23:46 (See also Matthew 27:50 and Mark 15:37, where Jesus dismisses his spirit.)*

What to look for in the events listed
- Look at the impact of each event on the people around Jesus.
- Notice where a gospel writer is the only one to record a particular event. Why do you think he included it? What does it add?
- Note that Jesus "said" seven things when he was on the cross (sometimes called his "seven words" from the cross). What does each reveal about Jesus?
- See how these events shed light on the words of Mark 10:45.

Concluding thought
- Some people say that at end of Jesus' life came as a result of "circumstances" (the Romans and the Jews), and as a consequence he was killed. But read Mark 8:31-9:1 and Mark 10:32-34, which show that Jesus foretold the details of his death.

See also: *Making study a spiritual exercise*, page 36.

"But the Bible's full of contradictions!"

It is no use pretending that there are no difficulties with the Bible. Some of the apparent contradictions are solved when we know more about the Bible; others may not be resolved in our lifetime.

The main purpose of the Bible is to teach us about God's love for us in his plan of salvation. It is not to satisfy other questions that we may have in our minds. The best way to cope with supposed contradictions in the Bible, is for us to know how to interpret them correctly in the first place.

Interpreting the Bible

What is the natural sense of the passage?

Christians believe that, "God is light; in him there is no darkness at all." (1 John 1:5.) So God reveals himself in the Bible in ways we can understand.

Sometimes this means that the correct way to interpret a Bible passage is in a figurative way, not in a literal way. This applies to certain types of literature, such as apocalyptic literature which reveals hidden truths, for example the Book of Revelation. There we read, "These ... have come out of the great tribulation; they have washed their robes and made them white in the blood of the Lamb." (Revelation 7:14.) It is impossible for robes which have been washed in "blood" to come out "white." John did not expect his readers to visualize this image, but to see it as a symbol.

Symbol	Interpretation
White robes	The righteousness of God's people.
The blood of the Lamb	The death of Jesus, which is totally responsible for bringing about the righteousness of God's people.
Washing robes	To wash a robe meant to put trust in Jesus.

When deciding how to interpret a passage in the Bible, ask yourself what the natural sense of the passage is – is it literal or figurative?

What is the general sense of the passage?

The Bible is in harmony with itself. When reading a verse or passage, we have to ask:

• How does it fit in with other teachings on the same subject in the Bible?

• What is its immediate context? (What is the subject matter of the paragraph, chapter and Bible book it is in?)

Do we have to believe that God literally wrote the Ten Commandments with his finger? Exodus 31:18 says, "When the Lord finished speaking to Moses on Mount Sinai, he gave him the two tablets of the Testimony, the tablets of stone inscribed by the finger of God."

What is the general teaching in the Bible about the finger of God?

People who talked about "the finger of God"	What they said
David	"When I consider your heavens, the work of your fingers." *Psalm 8:3*
Egyptian magicians referring (to the plague of gnats)	"The magicians said to Pharaoh, 'This is the finger of God.' " *Exodus 8:19*
Jesus (after he cast out demons)	"But if I drive out demons by the finger of God..." *Luke 11:20*

From these examples, we can conclude that the expression "the finger of God" is used in a special way in the Bible. It is a figure of speech meaning God's direct intervention.

Four interventions

• Intervention in creation: the heavens. *Psalm 8:3*

• Intervention in judgment: the plagues. *Exodus 8:19*

• Intervention in salvation: the exorcism of the demons. *Luke 11:20*

• Intervention in revelation: the giving of the law. *Exodus 31:18*

A year's worth of Bible studies

Opening observations

- Nearly everything we know about Jesus comes from the four gospels.
- Many people have set views about Jesus, but few of them have ever read the gospels.
- Spend an hour a week over the next year studying the life of Jesus in the four gospels.

Follow the life of Jesus in the table. Start by reading down one of the columns (Matthew, Mark, Luke and John), and looking up the Bible references. Complete Matthew before moving on to Mark, and so on.

A harmony of the four gospels

Topic	Matthew	Mark	Luke	John
Jesus' birth and childhood				
Jesus' family tree	1:1-17		3:23-38	
His birth	2:1-12		2:1-39	
Temple visit and childhood			2:40-52	
Preparing for public ministry				
Jesus' baptism	3:13-17	1:9-11	3:21-22	
Jesus' temptations	4:1-11	1:12-13	4:1-13	
Jesus starts his ministry				
John points to Jesus				1:19-34
Jesus' first "sign" (miracle)				2:1-12
Jesus meets Nicodemus				3:1-21
Jesus' work in Galilee				
Jesus' arrival in Galilee	4:12-17	1:14	4:14	4:43-45
Call of the twelve apostles	4:18-22	1:16-20	5:1-11	
The Sermon on the Mount	5:1-7:29		6:20-49	
Some of Jesus' parables	13:1-53	4:1-34	8:4-18	
Some of Jesus' miracles	8:23-9:8	4:35-5:43	8:22-56	
Jesus walks on the sea	14:22-33	6:45-52		6:16-21
Said to be the Christ	16:13-20	8:27-9:1	9:18-27	
Jesus' transfiguration	17:1-13	9:2-13	9:28-36	

Note what each gospel writer includes and leaves out.
• Ask yourself why a gospel writer tells a particular story in his gospel.
• What do the events tell us about who Jesus was?
• Note any differences between the gospel writers' accounts of the same incidents, and consider what these differences emphasize.

Topic	Matthew	Mark	Luke	John
Jesus' work in Judea				
Journey to Jerusalem	19:1-2	10:1	9:51-62	7:10
Jesus in Mary and Martha's home			10:38-42	
Jesus teaches a prayer			11:1-13	
Jesus brings Lazarus back to life				11:1-44
Jesus' journey towards Jerusalem				
The rich young ruler	19:16–20:16	10:17-31	18:18-30	
Jesus predicts his death	20:17-19	10:32-34	18:31-34	
Jesus arrives at Bethany				11:55–12:11
Jesus' last week				
Jesus enters Jerusalem	21:1-9	11:1-10	19:29-40	12:12-19
Jesus cleanses the Temple	21:12-16	11:15-19	19:45-48	
The widow's offering		12:41-44	21:1-4	
Teaching about the end	24–25	13:1-37	21:5-38	
The Passover meal	26:17-29	14:12-25	22:7-30	13:1-30
Peter's denial predicted	26:31-35	14:27-31	22:31-38	13:31-38
Jesus' final teachings				14:1–17:26
Jesus in Gethsemane	26:36-46	14:32-42	22:39-46	18:1
Good Friday	27:11-60	15:2-46	23:1-54	18:28–19:42
Resurrection appearances	28:9-20	[16:9-18]	24:1-49	20:1–21:23
Jesus' ascension		[16:19-20]	24:50-53	

15 ways to enhance your Bible study

Read to make you "wise for salvation"

Remember what the main purpose of the Bible is. It is not to acquire knowledge. According to 2 Timothy 3:15, Bible reading is *"to make us wise for salvation through faith in Christ Jesus."*

Don't be afraid to study the Bible

- Don't forget that you will get nowhere without relying on the Holy Spirit as you read, think, and study.
- Read through a different Bible book each month.
- Read one psalm every day.

Things to do

1 Compile your own biography. Find all the references you can to Peter in the New Testament. Make a list of the references. Write down one thing you learn about Peter's character next to each reference.

2 Read from a version of the Bible you have never used before.

3 Read one chapter from the New Testament in as many different Bible versions as possible.

4 Memorize verses. Memorize one Bible verse that has really helped you each week or month. Make a list of these verses and note down why you like them.

5 Read an Old Testament book you are unfamiliar with.

6 Watch a video about the Holy Land.

7 From the Book of Proverbs, compile a list of topics that are mentioned.

8 Use a computer. There are numerous software programs available. Your local Christian bookstore should be able to help you.

9 Buy a study Bible. These help you to understand the Bible better and better.

10 Join in with other people. Many churches and Christian organizations have Bible study groups, which can be very useful places for learning more about the Bible.

11 Read everything written in the New Testament by John. Start with John's Gospel, then his three letters, and finally the Book of Revelation.

12 Read John chapter ten alongside Psalm 23.

13 Each Christmas, ask for a present to help your Bible study.

14 Read a promise from the Bible before you go to sleep.

15 Listen to Handel's *Messiah*.

See also: *Making study a spiritual exercise*, page 36.